Dedication

To my daughter, Colleen Adaire Casey, the possessor of great fortitude—you are my heart.

INTRODUCTION

Hillary Clinton—you're either *for* her or you are **against** her. And if you're for her, you'll find an ample stockpile of reasons in this book to help you convince your friends, family, coworkers, and even complete strangers of why they should be, too. It's important that you're involved because Hillary is on a trajectory that will hopefully make her the most powerful person in the world for the next four years! Even Senator Lindsey Graham, who ran for a while in the Republican primaries, who doesn't like Hillary, who calls her the most dishonest person in America . . . even he thinks that she'll be the next president of the United States if she runs against Donald Trump. So this election matters. And if you care, you should read my books.

There's nothing *trivial* when it comes to deciding the next president of the United States. Your decision of whom to vote for in the 2016 campaign puts you in the *personal* mix for the future of yourself, your family, friends, and, most importantly, for America.

In trying to find the slippery and fragmented truth in this complicated political landscape, you have to blend public pronouncements and media coverage with personal feelings. It's hard to speak softly, to think before you shout. Normally I'm not one to orate on national politics from the top of Mount Pundit, but when you write about politics, you're forced to raise your voice. And it also helps to have a sense of humor.

Politics is big business. Most politicians acknowledge that, at least privately. And like all businesses, politics has specific rules of the roads, paths, and processes. These affect how candidates are perceived and elected, who gets into office, or who falls by the wayside. So if one aims to be the next president of the United States, she not only needs to be a great speaker and motivator, but an expert on how the political system works and how this affects voter choices. No one understands those key points better than Hillary Clinton.

All her angles, aspects, and strategies are covered. She not only plays the game, but she's the referee and also the fan in the stands. She's *that* good at what she does best—being a longtime successful politician in the limelight. She's a rabble rouser and crowd pleaser with whomever she's in front of. There's *no* denying that.

All voters make decisions, but so many make choices based on things as trivial as a candidate's untimely smirk, or sweat in front of a camera, or hairdo, or clothes. Sadly, many voters vote **against** one candidate more than **for** another. Many voters form their opinions on national political figures for purely personal or outrageously partisan reasons. That *seems* to be human nature.

Here in these pages I've given you 101 solid reasons to vote for her. They are not listed in any order of priority. The 1–101 numbering simply helps as reference points. Whatever your feelings toward Hillary Clinton, these reasons will better prepare you to participate in the upcoming battle to choose the next president of the United States of America.

Your opinion and vote *truly* matter.

Wilson Casey
Spartanburg, SC
TriviaGuy.com

P.S. For the well-rounded picture, be sure to check out my other work, ***101 Reasons to Vote Against Hillary Clinton***, covering the other side of Hillary Clinton's political coin. Thanks, and happy voting!

101

REASONS TO VOTE

FOR

HILLARY

1. It's tempting to say - why bother with a convention? We've waited long enough. Conventions just keep coming whether we want them or not, just like phone books. Hillary Clinton as "Madame President" has a good ring to it, the same nice caliber as Bill being called the "First Gent." Or perhaps "Vote for the First Dude" is a bumper sticker waiting to happen.

2. Hillary Clinton stands out for boldly fighting for expanding access to birth control and family planning. She has said, "You cannot have maternal health without reproductive health. And reproductive health includes contraception and family planning and access to legal, safe abortion." During her time in the Senate she worked to expand access to family planning and ensured that low-income women and those serving in the military had access to birth control. She achieved a 100 percent rating on the Planned Parenthood Action Fund scorecard while she was a senator.

3. She has an excellent resume and, without question, is the most talked-about woman in politics. No matter what you think of her, she has a lot of political experience. She was eight years the first lady during Bill's presidency, the first female senator from New York, and secretary of state during Obama's first term in office.

4. She knows what she wants: "Let me say this: hypothetically speaking, I really do hope that we have a woman president in my lifetime. I suppose I could have stayed home and baked cookies and had teas, but what I decided to do was to fulfill my profession, which I entered before my husband was in public life. God bless the America we (as Democrats) are trying to create."

5. If you've loved Obama's eight years in the White House, why not keep a good thing going? She's a strong advocate that more can be done to help the middle class and will be ceaseless in implementing ways to make housing more affordable, and to help younger Americans find more and better jobs.

6. Progressives have bashed her support of Wall Street, hinting she cares more about the middle class. That's simply not the case. She wants both to prospe: "The question should be how do we get a Main Street thriving and doing well, and how do we get a responsible Wall Street that is stimulating jobs? It's not an either-or."

7. She has a sense of humor. In an "A" or "B" quiz from a March 2016 radio show (Idaho's Mix 106) she showed her lighter side. The questions: (1) On a laid-back night at home, pizza or burgers? (2) For your birthday, gift card or something more personalized? (3) When watching Charlotte (granddaughter), follow the rules of mom and dad, or take grandparent liberties? Hillary's answers: (1) Pizza, (2) Personalized, (3) Liberties (but don't tell my daughter). She was also asked her favorite romantic comedy. Her answer: *The Princess Bride* (1987). OMG (oh my gosh), she's human after all.

8. The Supreme Court has leaned too far to the right for far too long. With Hillary as president she'll be able to choose justices more reflective of who we are as a people. In fact, she's open to the idea of nominating Barack Obama to the US Supreme Court. When it was suggested to her at a campaign event in Iowa (January 2016) she responded, "Wow, I love that, wow. He may have a few other things to do, but I tell you, that's a great idea. He's brilliant and he can set forth an argument and he was a law professor. He's got all the credentials." Obama taught constitutional law at the University of Chicago and was the first black president of the *Harvard Law Review* when he attended Harvard Law School. Hillary went on to say, "We need new justices who actually understand the challenges we face."

9. She's a strong woman, "We need to understand that there is no formula for how women should lead their lives. That is why we must respect the choices that each woman makes for herself and her family. Every woman deserves the chance to realize her God-given potential."

10. Hillary Clinton is a woman of her word. Since taking office in 2009 as the United States secretary of state, she repeatedly stated over the years that she was only interested in serving one term in that position. She officially stepped down from that post on February 1, 2013, with the conviction that she left the State Department and our country safer, stronger, and more secure.

11. You can see from her tweets on Twitter that she can balance many roles: wife, mom, lawyer, women and kids advocate, FLOAR, FLOTUS, US senator, secretary of State, author, dog owner, and TBD (to be determined) by your vote. She understands the work that needs to be done. She said, "It took a Clinton to clean up after the first Bush, it may take another Clinton to clean up after the second one."

12. She is strongly committed to making sure that every eligible American has the right to vote in fair, accessible, and credible elections. In 2005 Hillary Clinton introduced a piece of legislation called the "Count Every Vote Act" to provide a verified paper ballot for every vote cast in electronic voting machines. That's to ensure that all Americans are able to cast a free and unfettered vote, and that it be fairly counted. She is for same-day registration, earlier absentee voting, and desires to end the disparities in resources at voting precincts. Hillary Clinton is also open to the idea to try for a holiday or a weekend for voting so more people will be able to get off work and actually do it. She continues to push for a voter registration overhaul to improve our system of voting.

13. From her 2003 book *Living History*, Hillary Clinton believes even welfare children are better off with their parents. Poverty is not a disqualification from good parenting. Financial and social support for families with special problems should be a first step before giving up on them and taking away their children. The government should not intervene unless the children are endangered by abuse and neglect. She is against legislation that punishes children for circumstances beyond their control.

14. Hillary Clinton's will is extraordinary because she has taken many punches and continues to bounce back. Her advice is, "Take criticism seriously, but not personally. If there is truth or merit in the criticism, try to learn from it. Otherwise, let it roll right off you. Too many women, in too many countries speak the same language, of silence. Every moment wasted looking back keeps us from moving forward."

15. Did you know Hillary Clinton won a Grammy Award in 1997? She was awarded a Grammy in the Best Spoken Word or Non-musical Album category for the audiobook version of her bestselling book, *It Takes a Village*, in which she presented her vision for a society that meets all of a child's needs for better or worse.

16. Hillary Clinton has spent her life advocating on behalf of women and has continually tried to make work places, including all the ones she's been associated with, friendlier to women with children. She's been a hands-on mother to daughter Chelsea, and yet ever committed to her work ethics. She's a living example of being able to burn the candle at both ends, and to balance her work as a dedicated public servant with her responsibilities to her family.

17. Hillary Clinton on TV's *The View* (April 2016) stated she believes women can be both feminists and "pro-life." She said it's "absolutely" possible and explained why she doesn't think the two terms are mutually exclusive. "I respect the opinions and beliefs of every woman. The reason why being pro-choice (referring to abortion) is the right way to go is because it is a choice, and hopefully a choice that is rooted in the thoughtfulness and the care that women bring to this decision." Hillary has long been pro-choice as politicians continue to fight over issues such as access to birth control. She has also stated the potential for life begins at conception, but the lives of others involved with the decision to have an abortion are more important than the potential life. During her 2012 remarks at the Women in the World Summit (Washington, DC) she warned that "extremists" are out to control women and the United States "needs to set an example for the entire world" and "reject efforts to marginalize any one of us." That means keeping the government out of the abortion issue.

18. Hillary served eight years (1993–2001) as the First Lady during a decade-long economic expansion that stands as the longest period of growth in our history. During that tenure there was a gain of nearly 21 million jobs. No, she wasn't the president, but as first lady and first confidant and advisor she certainly played a role in the largest deficit reduction plan in history that reduced the deficit by $600 billion.

19. In March 2016 the American Nurses Association (ANA) endorsed Hillary Clinton. Its president, Pamela F. Cipriano, announced, "Hillary Clinton has been a nurse champion and health care advocate throughout her career and believes empowering nurses is good for patients and good for the country. We need a president that will make it a priority to transform the country's health care system into one that is high quality, affordable, and accessible." ANA represents the interests of the nation's 3.4 million registered nurses and endorse candidates who it feels have demonstrated strong support to best serve the interests of nurses and patients.

20.
She's the very notion of decisiveness. This is not because she's not liberal, but whereas Obama is more process-oriented, she is more action-oriented. Clinton's allies cringe at the notion she's labeled as a "hawk." Instead, they understand that she takes aggressive approaches and is strong-willed.

21. In a formal announcement in March 2013, she stated that she now believes gay people should be allowed to marry. This is a major reversal of a position she'd held for decades. Her counterparts highly criticized her for jumping on the bandwagon only after gay marriage had become more vocal and accepted. Hillary Clinton defended herself as a "thinking human" who is allowed to "evolve" on important issues.

22. Hillary Clinton believes that Americans shouldn't torture people. After a statement from the Senate Intelligence Committee in December 2014 on torture tactics, she stated, "The US should never condone or practice torture anywhere in the world." The documents were a condemnation of the torture tactics deployed in the fear-laden days and years after the September 11, 2001, terrorist attacks.

23. If lawmakers get a raise, so should others. Hillary Clinton believes the federal government should raise the minimum wage. She proclaims, "[Don't] let anyone tell you that raising the minimum wage will kill jobs—they always say that." She has repeatedly proposed legislation that would automatically increase the federal minimum wage any time members of Congress swell their own salaries.

24. Clinton believes that the United States should not trust Russian President Vladimir Putin. She calls him an arrogant bully. As Secretary of State she was in favor of Obama's "reset" policy with Russia. She has compared Putin's aggression in Ukraine to actions taken by Nazi leader Adolf Hitler outside Germany in the 1930s' prior to World War II. She still hopes for the best from Putin, and hopes to not have to change actual US policy toward Russia.

25. Clinton believes that the United States needs serious immigration reform. First, she would work with our Mexican neighbors to help them create more jobs and more opportunities for their own people. Second, she wants to bring the immigrants that are already in the United States out of the shadows and provide them with expectations that should be met on their path to legalization, such as paying a fine for coming here illegally, paying back taxes owed, and learning English.

26. "If we get a good deal, we should negotiate with Iran," Hillary claims, even at the vexation of the pro-Israel crowd. She supports talks with Tehran over its nuclear program and is credited with initiating the secret talks in 2012. She is forthright on cautioning the United States to be extremely clear about what it concedes to, reiterating that no deal is better than a bad deal.

27. She understands there's a process to making nuclear power an alternative energy source, but, she says, "I'm agnostic about nuclear power. Until we figure out what we're going to do with the waste and the cost, it's very hard to see nuclear as a part of our future. But that's where American technology comes in. Let's figure out what we're going to do about the waste and the cost if we think nuclear should be a part of the solution."

28. Throughout her career, Hillary Clinton has been a strong ally and representative of the Jewish community. She is an unwavering supporter of Israel's safety and security: "Israel and the United States are united by a deep and unbreakable bond based on mutual interests and respect." This steadfast support has never wavered.

29. Mrs. Clinton gave unwavering support for the raid into Pakistan to get Osama bin Laden, while President Obama was making up his mind whether to issue the order or not.

30. Barack Obama says voters want a "new car smell" in the 2016 White House race and acknowledges that Hillary Clinton won't agree with him on everything. It would be great to elect the perfect presidential candidate. Unfortunately, that's never been possible, nor ever will be. Hillary Clinton is the best alternative from imperfect candidates. She's had a front-row seat to one of the most prosperous periods in recent history.

31. Hillary Clinton supports public school choice and charter schools. She believes parents deserve greater choice within the public school system to address the unique needs of their children. Charter schools are publicly funded, privately run, and usually adhere to fewer district rules that stifle innovation than regular public schools. Hillary Clinton believes the charter school movement is one of the ways to continue positive turnarounds for the betterment of the entire public school system. She finds favorable persuasion of returning control from bureaucrats to parents and teachers. That empowers educators and system-raising academic standards for America.

32. She has wide demographic appeal groups. Even apart from Democrats and liberals, she has good numbers of support from nonwhites, moderates, younger and lower-income adults, post-graduates, and women. She also has cross-party appeal, as about a quarter of Republicans think she'd make a good president. Joe Biden says Hillary Clinton is "really a competent, capable person and friend."

33. Hillary Clinton is formidably making her case as to why she's right to serve as president, and not just basing her argument on "inevitability" or her right as a female political star. She now presents a warmer and more relatable side to voters.

34. Her dedication to our nation's servicemen and women is unquestionable. While a US Senator, Hillary Clinton introduced the Heroes at Home Act to help family members care for those with traumatic brain injury. She fought to increase the military survivor benefit from $12,000 to $100,000 and co-sponsored support for the Injured Service Members Act and to extend benefits under the Family and Medical Leave Act. Her record also indicates she's been an advocate for expanded health benefits for National Guard and Reserve members. In a 2007 speech to the Veterans of Foreign Wars she said, "The history of America is forged and sanctified by the men and women who loved their country enough to sacrifice their lives for it. You and your fallen comrades know that in the face of tyranny, cruelty, oppression, extremism, sometimes there is only one choice. When the world looked to America, America looked to you. And you never let her down."

35.

The last secretary of state to be elected to the nation's highest office was James Buchanan in 1856. Hillary will restore an old historic pattern of six previous secretaries of state (Thomas Jefferson, James Madison, James Monroe, John Quincy Adams, Martin Van Buren, and James Buchanan) who became president. Being the former secretary, she brings a wealth of knowledge and international experience to the White House. Foreign dignitaries and heads of government reassuringly know her, as she holds the record (112) for most countries visited in a secretary's tenure. She did so while proudly serving under President Barack Obama with the goals of preserving the national security of the United States, promoting world peace and a secure global environment, maintaining a balance of power among nations, working with allies to solve international problems, promoting democratic values and human rights, and furthering cooperative foreign trade and global involvement in international trade organizations.

36. Her view on abortion: "I have said many times that I can support a ban on late-term abortions, including partial-birth abortions, so long as the health and life of the mother is protected. I've met women who faced this heart-wrenching decision toward the end of a pregnancy. Of course it's a horrible procedure. No one would argue with that. But if your life is at stake, if your health is at stake, if the potential for having any more children is at stake, this must be a woman's choice."

37. Hillary Clinton's belief in religious values began early in life at age thirteen, as she made a commitment of faith at her United Methodist Church in Park Ridge, Illinois. After marrying Bill Clinton, a Southern Baptist, she joined and stayed active in a Methodist church in Little Rock, Arkansas. As first lady and later secretary of state, she attended Foundry United Methodist Church in Washington, DC.

38. In the past two elections of 2008 and 2012 America elected a man (Obama) who preached a message of "Hope" and "Yes We Can." The facts resoundingly declare, "We Must Continue." The time is now for Hillary to triumph and conquer our country's challenges regarding national debt, the economy, military might, unemployment, social issues, combating terror, and countless others. "We Must Continue. Elect Hillary."

39. In regard to affirmative action, Hillary believes equal pay is not yet equal. She wants to redress past discrimination against women and minority groups, and would like to improve their economic and educational opportunities. On looking at the opportunity gap, she says we've come a long way but still have a long way to go. She further has added, "The march is not finished and we Democrats call on everyone to be foot soldiers in that revolution to finish the job."

40. Hillary's beliefs in civil rights go back to 1962 when she briefly met Martin Luther King Jr. after his sermon, "Sleeping through the Revolution," in Chicago. In that speech he said that too many Americans were like Rip Van Winkle snoozing through the changes happening around them. Later in life, Hillary would comment that King's sermon opened her eyes as a teenager to other people and the way they live.

41. Hillary Clinton chaired the American Bar Association's Commission on Women in the Profession when it was first created in 1987. She set the pace of the organization by reporting that women are not advancing at a satisfactory rate. She maintains that barriers should be eliminated and a thorough reexamination of the attitudes and structures in the legal profession is needed. In 2013, Hillary Clinton was bestowed the ABA Medal, the organization's highest honor.

42. In a 2013 press release, ABA President Laurel Bellows said Hillary Clinton's career in law and public service inspires "generations of young women as they walk through the doors that she opened for them." Among Clinton's accolades: she was the first female full partner in her law firm, the first female chairperson of the board of directors of the Legal Services Corporation, and the first female US senator from New York.

43. Hillary continues to push for advances on affordable child care and paid family leave that could create greater economic progress for women. She realizes how tough it is for women to balance a demanding job while trying to raise young children. She pursues policy changes to give women "a fair shot." Hillary is tired of expanded, paid family leave plans stalling in Congress and will do something about it.

44. Hillary Clinton is very effective when on the defensive. "When you are attacked you have to deck your opponent," she's joked. A lot of blows keep coming her way. She swats them off while swinging back hard herself. She stays above the fray, but is always ready and adroit for the zinging back-and-forth one-liners among America's political parties.

45. She's the "Bill Clinton" of this century. She inspires.She's authentic. She's passionate. She wants to run the government like a start-up—with it being totally transformational. She campaigns on the premise that this election is truly about the voters, not her, not Obama, not Washington, but you.

46. Hillary Clinton will get some Republican votes. She has a familiar face on Wall Street following her tenure as a New York senator. Her moderate views on taxation and financial regulation in the big money world of the Republican elite are the most appetizing alternative to any Republican party nominee. Hillary Clinton believes banksters are necessary, not parasites.

47. All American kids should get free, high-quality pre-K education. Research findings suggest that by the time children turn four years old, the ones growing up in upper- and middle-class homes hear thirty million more words than kids whose families are on welfare. Hillary has declared, "Coming to school without words is like coming to school without food or adequate health care. It should spur us to action just like child hunger and child poverty."

48. Hillary Clinton stresses how important women are to our nation: "Reach out particularly to every single woman you know, because women's rights are like the canary in the mine. If you don't protect women's rights at home and around the world, everybody's rights are at risk." She also added, "When women vote in America, America wins." Her message resonates with women of multiple demographics: unmarried women, older women, and married ones, too. A pollster's findings said women feel she does understand the day-to-day challenges women face such as paying for kids' classes, getting everyone fed, handling a husband's job loss, etc. Women feel they have a sincere voice in Hillary Clinton.

49. Over the past 100-plus years, history has shown that the US economy, stock prices, and corporate profits have generated stronger growth under Democratic leadership in the White House. The S&P (Standard & Poor's Financial Services) 500 has rallied an average of approximately 12% per year since 1901 when Democrats occupy the White House, compared with around 5% for the Republicans. The best block of market performance since 1900 occurred in 1993–2000 under Bill Clinton when the S&P 500 rallied an average of 19.9% per year. For Republicans, the strongest market action occurred from 1981-1992 when the S&P 500 climbed an average of 13.5% each year under Ronald Reagan and George H. W. Bush. On doing the 100-year-old trending math, the gross domestic product increased when Democrats ran the executive branch, and there's also a disparity showing corporate profits are up during Democratic administrations. Electing Hillary means stronger growth trends in the vital areas for our country's future.

50.
Hillary Clinton is skilled in emotional intelligence. To describe her, words and phrases such as *sincere* and *transparent* are often used. She adheres to President Lyndon B. Johnson's theory, "If you had access to the same information I have, you'd make the same choices and decisions."

51. The late British Prime Minister Margaret Thatcher may have been called the "Iron Lady," but Hillary Clinton is the "New Iron Lady." In our era of politics in which spin seems to take precedence over substance, Hillary Clinton is an icon for what politics should be about—courage, spirit, and the determination to change things for the better.

52. From her book, *It Takes a Village*: "The unfettered free market has been the most radically disruptive force in American life in the last generation . . . [T]here's got to be a healthy tension among all of our institutions in society, and that the market is the driving force behind our prosperity, our freedom in so many respects to make our lives our own but that it cannot be permitted just to run roughshod over people's lives as well."

53. Hillary Clinton is a mainstream left-of-center Democrat and would facilitate a generational ideological shift while extending Barack Obama's legacy. However, she's no clone. That was proven when they battled each other in the 2008 Democratic primaries. Since she is not known as Barack's clone, she can distance herself from any unpopular aspect of Obama's terms as president. She's her own trailblazer!

54.
A dark little secret: some Republicans on Wall Street like Hillary Clinton. She is the only grown-up in the room. She supported big banks while she was in the Senate and also the war in Iraq. Wall Street does not want potential extremes on either side, so she has the balance they need, too.

55. Ever since the September 11, 2012, attack of a United States outpost in Benghazi (Libya) that left four Americans killed, questions have continued to arise over the role of then-Secretary of State Hillary Clinton. The tragic event was not formally labeled a terrorist attack of which Republicans and some media outlets put forth the notion there was a cover-up by the secretary of state and the Obama administration. The claim was that proper security warnings were not heeded before the attack, which led to military support coming too late. Hillary Clinton did take responsibility for the security or lack thereof at the compound. During a CNN interview she said, "I'm in charge of the State Department's 60,000-plus people all over the world, 275 posts. The president and the vice president wouldn't be knowledgeable about specific decisions that are made by security professionals. They're the ones who weigh all of the threats and the risks and the needs, and make a considered decision." Since the Benghazi terrorist strike, investigations have detailed failures on the US intelligence community, including a Senate Intelligence Committee report (January 2014). In it, there was only one specific reference to Hillary Clinton throughout the entire report. She was doing her job.

56.
Hillary Clinton has been a longtime advocate of the death penalty in a very few federal cases. During a debate in New Hampshire (February 2016) she said, "What I hope the Supreme Court will do is make it absolutely clear that any state that continues capital punishment must meet the highest standards of evidentiary proof of effective assistance of counsel. I have much more confidence in the federal system, and I do reserve it for particularly heinous crimes in the federal system, like terrorism. I thought it was appropriate after a very thorough trial that Timothy McVeigh received the death penalty for blowing up the Federal Building in Oklahoma City, killing 168 people, including 19 children in a daycare center." She has supported legislation to address racial profiling and is against mandatory minimums in that they are widely used to have a discriminatory impact. Hillary also believes we need diversion, like drug-specific courts with nonviolent offenders not serving hard time in our prison system. She wants more second-chance programs and stricter punishments for sex offenders and additional protections for children.

57. Hillary Clinton believes that Social Security is one of the greatest inventions in American democracy, and will do everything possible to protect and defend it. She supports retaining the Social Security tax cap. That makes income in excess of $102,000 untaxable. She has called repealing the Social Security tax cap a "tax increase on the middle class." She has also stated it'd be a risky scheme to try to privatize Social Security.

58. Her beliefs in medical marijuana are moderate: "I don't think we've done enough research yet, although I think for people who are in extreme medical conditions and have anecdotal evidence that it works, there should be availability under appropriate circumstances." She has also said, "I think we need to be very clear about the benefits of marijuana use for medicinal purposes."

59. While gun control issues are still pretty much the subject of congressional legislation, Hillary Clinton doesn't dispute Americans' rights to own guns. But she denounces the idea that anybody can have a gun, anywhere, at any time. She doesn't believe that is in the best interest of the majority. She further believes access to guns in the United States has grown way out of balance.

60. In her book *Hard Choices,* Hillary Clinton admits that she got Iraq wrong in agreeing with President Bush. She said, "Iraq was a mistake. I gave the benefit of the doubt in an area where I should not have, and then the initial decision was wrong, and then the follow-up that they did inside Iraq made it even worse." She believes we need to have a nonpartisan approach, whatever the problem.

61. Hillary Clinton urges governments to fight online campaigns aimed at recruiting for extremist movements spreading in the Muslim world: "We still have to do a better job protecting online space, including websites and chat rooms where extremists inspire and recruit followers." She wants to stop the spread of an "ideology of hate" by advocating for nations and democracies to do more to stop online recruiting.

62. Mrs. Clinton has lived in Washington, DC, and worked in federal government, so she knows how the city and government works. Unlike Bush, she won't be dependent upon anyone to teach her.

63. She co-sponsored the Innocence Protection Act that requires DNA testing for all federal executions. This act will help reduce the risk that innocent persons may be executed. It also prohibits a state from denying a prisoner DNA testing on death row if certain conditions apply. The Act established the National Commission on Capital Representation.

64. Hillary Clinton believes that women should register for selective service when they turn eighteen years old just like men currently do. She is opposed to a draft but thinks it fair to call upon every young American. She also believes that our all-voluntary military has performed superbly and doubts we'll ever have to go back to a draft.

65. Her "Student Borrower Bill of Rights" has language to revisit bankruptcy protections, refinancing rights, and limitations on how much a borrower can be forced to pay on their loans. She also wants to forgive student loans for universal national service, as she has introduced legislation for a public service academy.

66. Hillary Clinton desires to help what have been dubbed the "Beyoncé voters," a new demographic of voters who are single women: "I think what you have to do is make the case that Congress has an enormous impact on matters that are important to you. If you are worried about your student loan, saving for a house, worried about the conditions in the workplace, it's not just the president you elect, it's who you elect to Congress."

67. When asked by a reporter, based on what she has seen, what is the best and worst thing about being president, she replied: "The best thing is you can help people solve their problems and manage difficult situations. The worst thing is it's a never-ending, daunting set of responsibilities that 24/7 is not enough time to deal with."

68. "Probably my worst quality is that I get very passionate about what I think is right. It's time that we move from good words to good works, from sound bites to sound solutions. "The only experience in life that's not overrated: being a grandmother."

69. Hillary Clinton wants more resources and extra monies to fund first responders to homeland security. She says, "If you believe in homeland security without funding first responders, it's like saying you believe in building a hospital without doctors and nurses." She further adds, "If we don't better fund our first responders, we're not funding our first line of defense."

70. A country's trade balance is an essential economic indicator; a nation that is exporting much more goods than it is importing is in good economic strength. Hillary Clinton will require that all future trade agreements contain strong and enforceable labor and environmental provisions protecting our workers.

71. In regard to having gambling casinos, Hillary Clinton supports an individual state's judgment. Regulations are determined by the states, not the federal government. In an attempt to boost a local economy, often a state will seek a casino because a neighboring state has one with revenues being lost over the state line. Casinos earn tax revenue, create temporary jobs during construction, and also create permanent jobs to operate the casino.

72. She is for an "International Code of Conduct for Outer Space Activities" in that the long-term sustainability of human space-flight and satellite systems is at serious risk from space debris and irresponsible actors. Voluntary rules of the road and norms of behavior in space should be aimed at enhancing safety, due diligence, and transparency.

73. Military action is critical to the US-led fight against Islamic state militants in Iraq and Syria (ISIS). She says it is essential to try to prevent their further advance and their holding of more territory. She further believes military action alone is not sufficient. The fight is a long-term commitment. Hillary suggests, "We have to fight an information war as well as an air war."

74.
Clinton embraced the Obama administration's move to normalize relations with Cuba, saying, "Isolation has only strengthened the Castro regime's grip on power." he continues praising a relaxed US policy towards Cuba that solidifies support among the growing population of Latino voters. It also appeals to voters in farm states like Iowa eager to do business in Havana. Her view is that the US should lift its embargo on the island nation.

75. Hillary had Republican parents. While she was a college student, the Vietnam War changed her outlook and she became a liberal Democrat. She opposed that war and argued there should be limits on American power and the defense and intelligence agencies that manipulate it. She confirmed her newfound political viewpoints by supporting the anti-war campaign of Senator Eugene McCarthy in his bid to displace President Johnson as the Democratic nominee.

76. When she was twelve years old, she wrote to NASA inquiring how she could become an astronaut. NASA replied they didn't accept women into the astronaut program. Her mother comforted the young Hillary by saying her eyesight was much too bad anyway. In the class of 1965 at Maine Township High School South, Hillary Rodham was voted "Most Likely to Succeed." She impersonated herself on *Saturday Night Live* and is not afraid to laugh at herself. Her funny quirks include putting Tabasco sauce on everything—even salad!

77. Schools should allow student prayer, but no religious instruction. That means students may participate as long as they do so in a nondisruptive manner when they are not occupied in school activities. Also, she believes students should be free to express their religious beliefs in school assignments. Schools may certainly teach about the Bible and morality codes, provided they remain neutral with respect to the promotion of any exacting religion.

78.
She supported legislation to criminalize desecration of the United States flag, but opposes a constitutional ban on flag attacks. In public statements she has compared the act of flag-burning and desecration to the "burning of a cross." She considers it a violation of federal civil rights law when the act is intended to intimidate any person or group of persons.

79. Ever since she was a little girl, she has felt the enveloping presence of God in her life. She says it has been a gift of grace that has been incredibly sustaining. Her faith has given her the confidence to make decisions that were right for her, whether anyone else agreed or not. Hillary Clinton is categorized as part of the religious left, where she feels the Holy Spirit is with her throughout her journey. Her political philosophy is inspired by the words of John Wesley (1703–1791), "Do all the good you can, by all the means you can, in all the ways you can, in all the places you can, at all the times you can, to all the people you can, and as long as ever you can."

80. When natural disasters in our country occur such as hurricanes, floods, fires, and so on, she would pursue an agenda as president to cut through the red tape. She'd deliver the promised federal assistance and get services running. She believes her federal commitment and meaningful federal aid would overcome these challenges.

81. Perhaps the constitution should say, "All men and women are created equal." The United States is one of the few countries in the world that has never had a woman chief executive. Great Britain's Margaret Thatcher was elected prime minister three times. Lots of countries have elected women presidents, such as Argentina, Brazil, Chile, Ecuador, Finland, Iceland, Ireland, Liberia, Nicaragua, and the Philippines, to name a few.

82. Back in April 2015 Hillary Clinton officially launched her presidential campaign with a produced video that made many of us feel better about ourselves, our country, and our way of life for a better future. She said, "I'm running for president. Everyday Americans need a champion, and I want to be that champion—so you can do more than just get by—you can get ahead." She has been the prohibitive favorite from Day 1 for the Democratic Party's nomination and will ride that champion mentality into the White House.

83. If you're in to A-List celebrities and think they know best when it comes to politics, here are some in Hillary's camp of support: Clay Aiken, Warren Buffett, Matt Damon, Leonardo DiCaprio, Morgan Freeman, Lady Gaga, Tom Hanks, Magic Johnson, Diane Kruger, Padma Lakshmi, John Legend, Jennifer Lopez, Willie Nelson, Jack Nicholson, Josh Peck, Katy Perry, Amy Poehler, Chris Rock, Steven Spielberg, Usher, Kerry Washington, Kanye West, Olivia Wilde, Jeffrey Wright, and Pharrell Williams. There are plenty more.

84. Hillary Clinton is an advocate of women's rights. Her quotes include, "There cannot be true democracy unless women's voices are heard. There cannot be true democracy unless women are given the opportunity to take responsibility for their own lives. There cannot be true democracy unless all citizens are able to participate fully in the lives of their country. Human rights are women's rights, and women's rights are human rights. Let us not forget that among those rights are the right to speak freely—and the right to be heard."

85. One of Secretary of State Clinton's greatest achievements is when she rolled out the US Global Health Initiative (GHI) in 2010. The initiative's efforts focused on building stronger and sustainable health systems; global health partnerships, and private-sector engagement. Implemented strategies included the improvement of medical facilities, reduction of the spread of HIV, and to lower infant and maternal mortality rates. The United States with Hillary Clinton's initiative decided to cut aid to fight specific diseases, instead rechanneling the directive to beef up health systems.

86. When the housing crisis broke in 2008, Hillary Clinton called for a freeze on foreclosures. Barack Obama said no. Clinton believed lenders should voluntarily embrace the freezes to prevent widespread defaults. She did not want to impose the freezes through the force of law and wanted to create a $30 billion fund for states to deal with the effects of foreclosures. Her plan was to help individual homeowners pay their bills, and especially lost property tax revenues used for local police and firefighters. If she becomes president, she'll continue to look out for owner-occupied homes purchased with subprime mortgages.

87. Hillary is a realist. In watching her husband and President Obama campaign, she noted, "It is poetry. I get carried away and I've seen them a million times. That's not necessarily my forte. But I think what I've always been able to do is to really produce results in every job I've ever had. One of the funny things is that I have a whole archive of nice things Republicans have said about me. It's about working with me to find common ground. I love trying to help people. I was raised to believe you do all the good you can, to all the people you can, for as long as you can."

88. Hillary Clinton has the strength, courage, and right physicality to become president. She withstands the rigors of a campaign while remaining true to her convictions and emerges with dignity and grace. She regularly swims, walks, does yoga, and weight trains to stay healthy, along with eating lean proteins and plenty of vegetables and fruits. Perhaps her secret is that she eats at least one fresh hot pepper per day, a habit that started back in 1992 when husband Bill was running for president. She believes in its special immune-boosting characteristics that provide stamina and endurance while taking of herself on a demanding schedule.

89. At the Ohio State University for a Democratic town hall in March 2016, Hillary Clinton responded to a blunt question about the death penalty from Ricky Jackson, who was famously vindicated of a murder charge that left him on death row. In response she came out against the death penalty in almost all cases saying, "The states have proven themselves incapable of carrying out fair trials." She called for the elimination of the death penalty at the state level, but supports it at the federal level for terrorists and mass murderers like the Oklahoma City bomber and 9/11 hijackers.

90. The job of the first spouse or first gentleman is an important one. Hillary's husband,
Bill, is a former president of the United States
for two terms. If you can put aside his flaws,
infidelity, and past blunders, he'll now serve
as a public face for the White House who has
learned from his mistakes. Hillary will keep
him on a tight leash as the first spouse is ex-
pected to take an active role in social activism,
plus hold a significant advisory role and part.
How could he not? No one is better suited to
advise the president of the United States (Hillary), than a former president of the United
States (Bill). But she'll have the final say-so.

91. Republican Henry Kissinger, who was secretary of state and national security advisor under Presidents Nixon and Ford, said, "I've known her for many years now, and I respect her intelligence" (*USA Today* 2014). He also thought she ran the State Department in the most effective way that he'd ever seen. More effectively than himself? "Yes," he said with a smile. "I was more chaotic." In another interview (NPR 2014) he commented, "I know Hillary as a person. And as a personal friend, I would say yes, she'd be a good president (NPR 2014). . . . Yes, I'd be comfortable with her as president."

92. In 2012 Secretary of State Hillary Clinton and Foreign Minister Patricia Espinosa (Mexico) signed the Transboundary Hydrocarbon Agreement. It provided the groundwork for cooperation across some 1.5 million acres of shared oil and natural gas resources in the Gulf of Mexico. Before that, those million-and-a-half acres in that what they call the Western Gap part of the Gulf of Mexico was off limits. Nobody was producing. The agreement created guidelines for determining the scope of the deep-water fields and how companies acting on behalf of each country can work together to access these reserves.

93. In the current campaign Hillary Clinton has won endorsements from at least 40 US senators, 13 former senators, and more than 100 House members. Critics of these facts would boast she's definitely part of the Washington establishment. Deservedly so, as there would be less political paralysis in the nation's capital. She's vastly worked with many on both sides of the aisle. A vote for her is far more likely for her as the president to get things done. A case in point: she worked with leaders of both parties in Congress to launch the Children's Health Insurance Program, providing health coverage to millions of children.

94. In January 2016 Hillary Clinton was asked some simple questions by Buzzfeed. Why are you doing this? What truly motivates you? "There is only this," coming from Hillary, "love and kindness." She expanded on that theme a few weeks later. "I want this campaign, and eventually my administration, to be more about inspiring young people, and older ones as well, to find that niche where kindness matters, whether it's to a friend, a neighbor, a colleague, a fellow student—whether it's in a classroom, or in a doctor's office, or in a business—we need to do more to help each other."

95. Obama has predicted the Cuban embargo will be lifted under his successor. Hillary Clinton strongly supports that concept and has said (July 2015, Florida), "Fundamentally most of the republican candidates still view Cuba and Latin America more broadly through an outdated Cold War lens. Instead of opportunities to be seized, they see only threats to be feared. They refuse to learn the lessons of the past or pay attention to what's worked and what hasn't. For them, ideology trumps evidence, and so they remain incapable of moving us forward. As president I would increase American influence in Cuba rather than reduce it. I would work with Congress to lift the embargo and I would pursue additional steps."

96. Hillary Clinton, while a senator, sponsored a bill for mental health service for older Americans. She called it the "Positive Aging Act." Although it never came to a vote, her remarks were that the bill was an effort to improve the accessibility and quality of mental health services for our rapidly growing population of older Americans. "We owe it to older adults in this country to do all that we can to ensure that high-quality mental health care is both available and accessible. In far too many instances our seniors go undiagnosed and untreated because of the current divide in our country between health care and mental health care. This legislation takes an important step in that direction."

97. She stands up for unions and wants to make sure the people who work hard every day can actually support their families and save for the future. Hillary Clinton understands there's a connection between unions and the middle class. She has voted YES on restricting employer interference in union organizing and wants to make sure unions can push for fair wages and good working conditions. She does not like employers who are illegally preventing workers from unionizing by using tactics that amount to harassment and firings. Current penalties to employers are so minor that they are ineffective deterrents. Hillary Clinton wants to change that.

98. She has proposed universal pre-kindergarten for every four-year-old. There are states that plan how many prison beds they will need in ten to fifteen years by looking at current third-grade reading scores (failure rates). Hillary Clinton would rather pay for pre-kindergarten than for more prison beds. She believes every young person in America has the right to a high-quality education that starts early to keep them on the right track. The evidence is overwhelming that pre-kindergarten will help children to stay in school longer, to do better, and to stay out of trouble.

99. Hillary Clinton pledged to "get to the bottom" of UFOs and aliens at a January 2016 campaign stop in New Hampshire. A Conway *Daily Sun* reporter reminded her that he had previously asked her about UFOs in 2007 and that she had said the number-one topic of freedom-of-information requests her husband received at his library was UFOs. Just prior to John Podesta being named as Hillary Clinton's campaign chairman, he publicly tweeted (after serving as Obama's advisor for a year), "My biggest failure of 2014: Once again not securing the disclosure of the UFO files." Hillary, given her relationship with Podesta, might be sincere enough to move forward with full UFO disclosure.

100. In 2014 Hillary Clinton's memoir, *Hard Choices*, which gave blow-by-blow accounts of tough discussions with Chinese officials, particularly on human rights, was blocked from being sold in China. One particular case of her fighting for human rights significantly added to the ban, as she personally intervened to help a blind dissident, Chen Guangcheng. The gentleman was seeking refuge in the United States Embassy in 2012 in Beijing. The embassy learned that he had escaped security guards in his village south of Beijing and was appealing to the Americans for help and sanctuary. The decision about what to do was passed up to Hillary Clinton, and on talking with her aides she said, "Go get him." In a justification she said his predicament represented all the United States stood for.

101. Even if you're a die-hard Republican, you might want to seriously consider voting for Hillary Clinton for president. In fact, you might be thinking about that already. Hillary has noted, "One of the funny things is that I have a whole archive of nice things Republicans have said about me. It's about working with me to find common ground. I love trying to help people. I was raised to believe you do all the good you can, to all the people you can, for as long as you can."

The reasons are numbered 1–101, but in no particular order as to priority. It's up to you, the reader, to pick out your favorites. Decide on your personal **TOP 10** reasons and list them! Have fun comparing with friends and family! See how many you agree on.

Want more? Create a list of additional reasons why Hillary should move back into the White House, this time as president.

Name: _____

Date: _____

My Top 10 Reasons   Ref.
                              in Book

#1 _____   _____

#2 _____   _____

#3 _____   _____

#4 _____   _____

#5 _____   _____

#6 _____   _____

#7 _____   _____

#8 _____ x _____   _____

#9 _____   _____

#10 _____   _____

Foreign Policy Reasons

#1 _____   _____

#2 _____   _____

#3 _____   _____

#4 _____   _____

#5 _____   _____

#6 _____   _____

#7 _____   _____

#8 _____   _____

#9 _____   _____

#10 _____   _____

National Security Policy Reasons

#1 _____ _____

#2 _____ _____

#3 _____ _____

#4 _____ _____

#5 _____ _____

#6 _____ _____

#7 _____ _____

#8 _____ _____

#9 _____ _____

#10 _____ _____

Social Policy Reasons

#1 _____   _____

#2 _____   _____

#3 _____   _____

#4 _____   _____

#5 _____   _____

#6 _____   _____

#7 _____   _____

#8 _____   _____

#9 _____   _____

#10 _____   _____

Health Care Policy Reasons

#1 _____   _____

#2 _____   _____

#3 _____   _____

#4 _____   _____

#5 _____   _____

#6 _____   _____

#7 _____   _____

#8 _____   _____

#9 _____   _____

#10 _____   _____

Economic Policy Reasons

#1 _____ _____

#2 _____ _____

#3 _____ _____

#4 _____ _____

#5 _____ _____

#6 _____ _____

#7 _____ _____

#8 _____ _____

#9 _____ _____

#10 _____ _____

Supreme Court Reasons

#1 _____ _____

#2 _____ _____

#3 _____ _____

#4 _____ _____

#5 _____ _____

#6 _____ _____

#7 _____ _____

#8 _____ _____

#9 _____ _____

#10 _____ _____

Gun Control Policy Reasons

#1 _____   _____

#2 _____   _____

#3 _____   _____

#4 _____   _____

#5 _____   _____

#6 _____   _____

#7 _____   _____

#8 _____   _____

#9 _____   _____

#10 _____   _____

Women's Rights Policy Reasons

#1 _____ _____

#2 _____ _____

#3 _____ _____

#4 _____ _____

#5 _____ _____

#6 _____ _____

#7 _____ _____

#8 _____ _____

#9 _____ _____

#10 _____ _____

Notes